THE
FREEDOM OF
FORGIVENESS

THE CORNERSTONE
PUBLISHING

TIMOTHY O. ABRAHAM

THE FREEDOM OF FORGIVENESS

ISBN: 978-1-944652-57-9

Cornerstone Publishing
A Division of Cornerstone Creativity Group LLC
Phone: +1(516) 547-4999
info@thecornerstonepublishers.com
www.thecornerstonepublishers.com

To order bulk copies of this book or to contact the author please call: (832)-287-2492
email: abrolus555@gmail.com

DEDICATION

I gracefully dedicate this book to God Almighty,
for His mercy and loving kindness in my life.

I thank Him for His grace to write this book.
Hallelujah!

CONTENTS

INTRODUCTION

If you do not know what it feels like to forgive, then you are missing out on a great deal in your life. You can make yourself psychologically stronger by learning to forgive and it's easier than you can ever imagine. As you read through this book, it is suggested that you take the lead by practicing the exercises that are mentioned within each of the chapters. Often times, people struggle to get past painful memories in their lives. Even though this is not something new and we all know that we should learn to forgive and forget since elementary school! Unfortunately, many people tend to dwell on the past and that only creates a downward spiral of pain and disappointments.

The book puts this in simple terms so that you are able to start off with letting go small things and work your way towards the bigger picture. Ultimately, what we truly yearn for is a sense of fulfillment and happiness in life. Holding grudges to your grave is not something you would wish for, both for yourself and even others. We only live once so don't leave behind disappointments and regrets. I was prompted to write down all that I know about forgiveness, so that others never have to go through the kind of tragic experience I witnessed.

Despite the general idea of forgiveness, which is "sacrificing" yourself for others, it is actually more than that. In fact, forgiveness is a "gift" that you give to yourself and people you love. You may not see it like this at the moment, but once you study what I'm about to share, you should be able to put negativity behind you and start to enjoy life to its full extent. Any kind of negativity will hold you back. Forgiveness is the life preserver every day offers you. It is your choice whether you take it, but once you do, you will understand how much it changes everything about your life and frees you from all of the pain and bitterness that come with it.

Chapter 1

FORGIVING OTHERS – WHAT IS TRUE FORGIVENESS?

―――――◇◇◇◇◇―――――

True forgiveness doesn't come back to kick you in the teeth. When you learn about forgiveness, it's like giving a gift. You give with no strings attached. People who say that they forgive but still bring up the past every time shows that they haven't truly forgiven. They might have said that they had forgiven but with zero intent. So, what is true forgiveness?

TRUE FORGIVENESS

Daisy is a gifted child. However, she mingled with the wrong kids who were into stealing and because she wasn't very good at it, she was caught. As expected, her parents were angry. After the entire saga, they encouraged her to move on and do better things in life. Verbally, they forgave her. Several years later, her mother was still constantly reminding the child of the thing that she did wrong every time she got mad. Of course, this didn't sit well with Daisy and she felt terrible every time her mother brings up the past. Furthermore, Daisy found that this stifled her creativity and that she dreaded going home to her mother because she knew that history would repeat itself. In the end, their relationship turned sour and things only got from bad to worse.

When you truly forgive someone, the past shall remain the past and should never be brought up again. Forgiveness gives both you and the person you feel has wronged you the freedom to move on. However, forgiving doesn't mean forgetting.

Daisy actually grew up to be a very forgiving person, learning from the lessons that she had been taught by her mother, and embraced with unconditional love. Even though you may remember the event as if it was yesterday, forgiveness means not bringing it up at a future time whenever you feel like it. You liberate yourself by learning to let go of blame and starting to embrace compassion. Let me give you an example:

John was always bullied by his brother. As he grew up, he had less to do with his brother but could see that his brother's life wasn't a very happy one. Instead of holding onto bad feelings, John learned that compassion was a better answer. He approached his brother to see if there was something he could do to help his brother through a bad patch. His brother was astounded that John would even bother with him after all the hell that he had put John through as a child, but when people forgive, it helps them to see things from both sides.

You have to remember that people who make your life a misery are usually quite miserable themselves. You have a choice to let go, and to forgive, or to carry a grudge and live with blame and anger. Both are bad for you because these are negative traits and they diminish who you are. Even if you were technically right in the 'blame game', deep inside you won't feel good due to all the negativity and sense of grudge.

FORGIVENESS REQUIRES THE STRENGTH OF CHARACTER

Forgiveness requires the strength of character, rather than weakness. Those who are able to forgive are more likely to live happier lives. In John's case, his brother is now his best friend because he learned from the kid he bullied how to move on and create major successes in life despite circumstances. John's brother asked him once how he could forgive and the answer is simple, to love is far better than to hate someone. He didn't despise him, or try to prove that he was better than his brother, but he demonstrated that when you forgive, you become a happier and more fulfilled human being. There is no better example than John himself.

There are so many things that people are unable to forgive from their childhood till death start knocking onto their door. That intangible burden that they carry with them their entire lives will diminish their ability to experience true happiness and fulfillment. This places a heavy burden not only on them, but also people around them. Forgiveness allows you to lift that burden and to see life from a different perspective. No matter what childhood offered or left in its tracks, forgiveness and acceptance of life is a healthier way to go and makes you less bitter. That bitterness tarnishes everything that you do and each interaction you have with others until YOU decide to let it go.

Remember that it's our responsibility to make the world a better place. Believe me, once you experience letting go, you will never go back to the bitterness again, because the choice is so much sweeter. It makes you feel like you have un-laden a huge load and when you feel that way for the first time, you will be shocked at how easy it is. It's not even about pride. It's about saying sorry and moving on in your life to start over with new hopes and dreams.

True forgiveness is when you can look inside and see no hatred, negativities or any strings attached to past bitter experiences. You begin to see the good in you and it isn't being vain or narcissistic. You'll be freed from the burden of all the bad things that happened and that truly is a gift that only those who are prepared to look beyond remorse and anger will experience. That, my friend, is the Freedom in Forgiveness.

Chapter 2

THE POWER OF FORGIVENESS AND HOW IT CAN BENEFIT YOU

When you are angry, it's hard to understand that forgiveness works two ways. It lets someone get away with actions that are unacceptable and that's the side that most people see, but there's much more to it than that. It lets you get away without all the bitterness. Let's look at the ways in which forgiveness helps you. After all, this is a fundamental benefit that you deprive yourself of if you cannot forgive:

What is The Difference Between Forgiving Someone and Condoning Their Actions?

There is a difference between forgiving someone and condoning their actions. There are a lot of kids today who had experienced child abuse at some point in their lives. So what happens to the upbringing of the child? There are only 3 possible outcomes: One is that they'll be totally broken down, afraid of their parents, and have low self-esteem.

The second possible outcome is that they'll hate their parents deep to the core, go against every word they say, and become a 'rebel' child. In the future, they might even follow their parents' footstep, thinking that "This is how it should be. I was brought up this way anyway!"

The third possible outcome is they simply forgive and learn from their experience. As a result, they could avoid the same mistake and shape their character into a more compassionate human being. It sure takes a lot of courage, but what you gain is so much more than what is lost. If you don't learn to forgive, you begin to be the perpetrator and the lack of forgiveness is every bit as wrong as holding onto the memory and allowing it to cloud your judgment in the future.

Studies that were done on forgiveness showed

there are other benefits as well. Forgiveness is good for your heart health. It helps you to lower high blood pressure because you are able to let go of the cause of that biochemical change in your body that anger and stress cause. There are so many stress related ailments these days and much of it is down to the way that you look at life. Compassionate people retain their innocence and can welcome the world with open arms, whereas those who cannot forgive will always put barriers between themselves and the world around them.

All religions and philosophies agree with the fact that forgiveness is valuable to your soul, or to the very way that you look at life and letting go allow you to reform relationships and make a real connection with the world.

SENSE OF EMPATHY

Forgiveness opens up the path to empathy. If you can't see the world through someone else's eyes, you limit your own viewpoint of life. Empathy makes you into a more complete person and helps you to peacefully co-exist with others whose opinions differ from your own. Since the whole world's way of living is based upon what people think, forgiveness frees you from the hold of anger and indignation. Thus, you see the world in a much broader perspective and are able to understand differences of opinion.

Forgiveness is extremely powerful. It enables you. It frees you from all of the negative feelings that you may go through as a result of being closed-minded. I remember someone that I knew taking up a new religion and being very devout. The one area that she had difficulty with was forgiveness. She had experienced bad things in her past that she could never let go of. When the friend who had betrayed her died, she found out too late that she could have forgiven and cherished a very valuable relationship. One small conversation stopped the relationship and in retrospect, she saw how petty and small that conversation was and yet it had eaten up years of what could have been a very productive and loving relationship. Standing at the grave of her old friend, she realized it was just too late, and now she has to live with all the regrets – until she could forgive herself for what she had done. The problem is that if you can't let go, the repercussion can actually be more serious than the actual event.

We all make mistakes, but they are only mistakes when they get in the way of relationships to the extent that you can never go back. It took her a long time to realize that forgiving herself was just as valuable as forgiving the friend who had wronged her.

The US National Library of Medicine has a wonderful piece that may be worth reading if you doubt the benefits of forgiveness. Their work involved a study of over 100 students and measuring the efficiency of their blood pressure and heart rate based upon their ability to forgive.

CHARACTER TRAITS

For those who are prepared to work on their character traits, there is an action that you can take to show you immediately what forgiveness does. The next time someone hurts you, don't wait for them to apologize. Break the ice and call them to get the relationship back onto a good footing. It really doesn't matter who apologizes first as long as there's forgiveness. The fact is that the person who cannot apologize is always going to be in a weaker position. If you take the initiative to make up with that friend, you show your strength of character and that can help that friend of yours to understand there are other ways to move forward in life.

Chapter 3

THE DANGER OF REFUSING TO FORGIVE

There are always going to be penalties of not being able to forgive. Let me give you an example.

THE POISON OF UNFORGIVENESS

Claire was once cheated on by her husband. She went forward in her life and because she held onto the anger, she took it into future relationships that could have worked out well for her. Before men were able to prove their love for her, her anger made her act in a way that actually drove them away.

You imprison your heart when you cannot forgive. Claire found herself going through the pockets of her partner. She found herself looking for problems even if there were none because she was unable to accept that people could be good to her. By doing so, she diminished herself and made herself less valuable as a partner.

Annie, on the other hand, looked at the situation from a different stance. She loved her husband and accepted – after the initial pain – that she had contributed in some way toward the breakdown of her marriage. Instead of being bitter, she used her experience to learn how to become a better person in the future. She was able to free herself of all of the negative connotations that are attached to blame, by using the negative experience to help her to grow emotionally.

THE IMPRISONMENT OF UNFORGIVENESS

When you cannot forgive, you imprison yourself, rather than the person you cannot forgive. You suffer from anger, hate, negativity, lack of trust and all of the things that make you less of a person. Even if you've had someone wrong you unjustly, if you can let go of all of these feelings, you become stronger without becoming hardened to life. You retain your innocence and learn that your method of dealing with negative emotions serves you in a much more positive way. If someone wronged you, don't let their wrong become yours. Let go and move on.

It's easier to succumb to addiction when you cannot forgive. You hide behind anti-depressants or maybe you turn to alcohol because it takes you out of that uncomfortable space YOU created for yourself. Those who are not compassionate see anger and resentment as a normal state of mind. The strange thing is that when you manage to let go of it, you change on the outside as well as the inside. You look happier and attract happier people into your life.

FALLING INTO DISTRACTIONS AND ADDICTIONS

The feeling that you have in your heart reflects on the outside and shows you how to be a compassionate and empathetic person, thus making you a better person. Hold onto the addictions that you use as a bolster against being hurt again and you create even more tension in your life and have more things to forgive or be forgiven for. It's a vicious circle and a glass of your favorite brew won't help you long term to change something within yourself that is fundamentally flawed. When you learn to forgive, you heal yourself from that damage.

The body of a human being is composed of energy. You must have felt that energy when you are in the company of people who are angry. The ideal scenario is to get as far away from that anger as you can. When you cannot forgive, you give off this negative energy and people around you will avoid you because of it. Even though you may have been the victim to something that you didn't even ask for, your victim status goes into overdrive when you cannot move on and forgive.

TO APOLOGIZE IS A SIGN OF STRENGTH, NOT WEAKNESS

One of the main reasons that people hold out for an apology is that they feel it vilifies the bad action on the part of the offender. The apology is the acknowledgement of wrongdoing. However, quite often in our lives, we see things that others don't see.

Ian explains this very well when he talks about his father. Ian felt most of his life that he didn't live up to the expectations of his father. The anger that he carried with him went on for years.

During the years of growing up, Ian wanted his father to apologize for all of the things he had put Ian through as a child. The fact was that Ian's father wasn't even aware that he had done anything wrong.

The fact is that people don't always realize their sins. Ian had built up this anger towards his father that was unreasonable. And here's the irony. When Ian himself became a father, he realized that he was doing the exactly same thing to his son. It wasn't ill treatment at all. These actions were taken out of care for his son.

When he managed to get all of this into

perspective and let go of his bitterness, he managed to forgive his father and attempt to make the relationship a much stronger one.

When you can't forgive, you make your own life a misery and much of the time, those who wronged you are quite happily going about their lives blissfully unaware of all of the negative thoughts you have in your mind. That's why it's so important to voice out and let go.

PUT YOURSELF IN SOMEONE ELSE'S SHOES

Try it today. Call someone who you have lost contact with simply because you could not forgive them. Make sure to focus the conversation around them, not you. You will begin to see that life isn't one dimensional. If you have problems with this exercise, then I would suggest that you to practice meditation because it will help you to let go of all of the negative feelings you feel toward life and see things from a different perspective.

You will become less introspective and will be

able to accept comments from others without laying judgment upon them. That helps you to be able to embrace compassion in a way you may not have been able to do before. When you do, your whole life changes for the better.

Chapter 4

FORGIVE NOT FORGET – LEARN FROM EXPERIENCE, NOT IGNORANCE

From a very young age, we form our behavior based on years of interaction with others, which includes our family, friends, and even strangers that we came across.

WE'RE INFLUENCED BY OUR SURROUNDINGS

We consciously or even subconsciously emulate the behavior of those we admire. At the same time, we try to avoid behavior of those we feel less comfortable with. But the big takeaway is, we're constantly striving to become the best version of ourselves. While you may not be able to forget what someone did that hurt you, you don't have to use this in a negative way. Instead, you can use all the past painful experiences and failures as a positive reinforcement to improve yourself.

BE MINDFUL OF WHO YOU WANT TO BE

The best strategy to discover the best version of you is to be mindful at all times. Be mindful of your current behaviors and decide whether each of these behaviors serves your higher purpose. Identify what behaviors you want to take on and what behaviors you should reject.

LEARN FROM EXPERIENCE

Also, learn from your past experiences. For instance, you forgive the bully at school and realize that his actions are not ones that you condone. Therefore, you know that bullying is bad and you will never be a bully. You forgive the person who isn't punctual and left you waiting idly for them. You now know how frustrated it is to wait for a person who's late and would never wish to impose that on anyone. Each of these things seems like common sense, but so many people hold onto grudges and learn nothing from them. Yes, you have the 'rights' to hate and even hold grudges, but think of the big picture. Instead of instilling hate, tell them what they did was wrong and move on, regardless of apology. You might feel like a loser in this situation but always look at the big picture. Forgiving others and moving on show your strength in character.

That's a precious lesson to learn. Thus, it's not a question of forgetting. It's a matter of putting that action into your mind and learning never to do that to others. Of course, don't let history repeats itself. Simply learn from experience and move on. That way, you enrich who you are and be a lot happier.

FORGIVING THYSELF

This also applies to when you need to forgive yourself. If you have done something to upset someone else, the best way forward is to be humble and apologize. Whether they accept your apology or not doesn't matter, it's all up to them. You cannot be responsible on how others deal with forgiveness. Focus on yourself first. If you have done all that you can to make amends, move forward and learn your lesson so that you don't make the same mistake again. Don't beat yourself up when you've done everything possible to make amends as it can never resolve anything. It is important that you are able to forgive yourself and release yourself from past attachments that can only bind you, and make you suffer.

THE PAST DOES NOT EQUAL THE FUTURE

Elisa was a victim of domestic violence in a failed marriage. Sadly, she had low self-esteem and by the end of her marriage, she still believed that she only got what she deserved. Fortunately, she managed to grow in character after being alone for a while. She realized that she held grudges both against her abusive husband for treating her like dirt as if she had no worth – and against herself because she hadn't lived up to his expectations.

After a long struggle, she was surprised that she was able to forgive him and let him know that she held no grudges against him and that she wished him well in his life. It made her feel whole again. It was like walking away with her head held high. She used empathy to try and see the situation from her husband's viewpoint, bearing in mind his background and his own demons in life. Then she had to take the walk toward forgiving herself for several things. Had you asked her what she had to forgive herself for, the answers would have been contradictory which is why she had so much trouble handling her feelings:

- She thought she had not lived up to what was expected of a wife.
- She thought that she was worthless for thinking all the bad thoughts about her husband.
- She also thought she wasn't worth much more than he had offered her.

However, as she went through the healing process, after forgiving herself, she found that she had to let go of her past and move on as the past does not equal the future. Today, she is able to form a strong foundation in her life, before embarking on another elationship.

There are women who believe that holding

onto past sins makes them attractive to men who enjoy protecting their other half. Often times, this is based upon not being able to forgive themselves and having lost their sense of self-esteem.

Unfortunately, these are the types of women who will walk from one abusive relationship to the next because they never form that strong foundation when they're single and rely on someone else for strength. That's a huge mistake. You have to find yourself, plant your roots and become a person you love and respect before you can expect to have that kind of love and respect from someone else. The truth is that we never really do forget about the things that people do that hurt us. However, when you're able to forgive, you can also learn how to make your life a much better place. Also, you'll discover how to approach life from a much more compassionate standpoint.

Chapter 5

WAYS TO ABSOLUTE FORGIVENESS

When something 'bad' happens that makes you mad, annoyed, and frustrated, don't let the emotions control you. Be the master of your emotions and don't react to the negative emotions. Instead, take a step back and calmly look at the situation as a whole. Then forgive others and look for solution in a positive state. You'd be surprise with the incredible outcome. Thus, before you're able to do this, you need to learn how to let go. This is something that was being taught in yoga and meditation. The benefit of these is that you are taught to be able to breathe in such a way that you're able to bring down your blood pressure and the rate of your heartbeat. As a result, you're able to look at this negative situation with an open mind. Meditation requires mindfulness, which is a crucial part of being able to let go. How much you suffer depends on how quickly you are willing to forgive fully.

HOW TO MEDITATE

The interesting part of meditation is that it teaches you how to let go of all thoughts and to give them no credence. As you ponder upon your life, you are subjected to all kinds of opinions. Thoughts come and go and you seem to have very little control over them.

However, when you meditate, you need to focus on your breathing. If your thoughts wander, you acknowledge the thoughts and simply let them go without allowing your emotions to take over. At the same time, you're practicing the principle of non-judgement. After all, it's just a thought and that's all there is to it. Of course, in the real world, it's easier said than done. But in meditation, you simply focus on your breathing.

Allow me to explain how meditation works because this will help you to achieve absolute forgiveness and detachment. Even when you are not meditating, you can distance yourself from negative thoughts by taking deep, mindful breaths.

Sit on a chair that gives you plenty of support. It's best to use a dining chair rather than something that you sink into because the straightness of your back is important. Your feet should be planted onto the floor and remain flat. Your hands are placed in your lap and your main hand is turned palm upward to receive the other hand – also palm upward, and you connect your thumbs together. Keeping your back straight, breathe in but instead of only using the top of your lungs like people normally do, you are expected to breathe in extra deeply until you feel the air in your upper gut. Hold onto it for a moment and then breathe out. You continue in this way, counting 8 for the inhale, 5 for the holding your breath and 10 for the exhale. During this exercise, your mind is busy with counting and concentrating on the breath, so you don't have time to think about anything else.

This is the bit that people find difficult, but

that's why they suggest that you practice meditation 20 minutes a day every day and make meditation part of your lifestyle. Practice makes perfect and it helps to discipline the mind. If you notice that there are thoughts popping up in your mind, don't resist them and realize that it's normal. Simply observe them, rather than submitting into your jumbled thoughts. See them, acknowledge that they are there and then let them go.

WHEN TO MEDIATE?

So here comes the most common question: When to meditate?

The best time of the day to meditate is first thing in the morning before breakfast or in the early evening on an empty stomach. The purpose of meditation is to learn how to let things go and when this practice has become a habit, you too can let go of any negative thoughts on a daily basis.

When you are learning to forgive, either yourself or someone else, you need to acknowledge the thoughts that you have and try to see them without all the emotions kicking in. Then let them go. You can get so much peace of mind as you free yourself from being caught up in situations and emotions. Meditation gives you the inner peace that helps you immensely in forgiving others and moving on rather than harboring bad feelings. Trust me, it feels refreshing and you'll be able to empathize others easily in that uplifting state.

ACHIEVING ABSOLUTE FORGIVENESS

When you wish to forgive someone, let them know that you forgive them and it's time to move on or reconcile. That should always be the end of the story.

You should never have to bring up the rotten past and remind others how they've wronged you especially when you're arguing. Otherwise, it isn't absolute forgiveness. Absolute forgiveness means that you are able to put all of that behind you and move on.

The same can be said when forgiving yourself. After you decide to let go of the past, never bring back those negativities and fuel your emotions. Be kind to yourself. Giving yourself absolute forgiveness is a great way to make you stronger and helps you to thrive in future relationships.

RELIGIOUS TEACHINGS ON FORGIVENESS

Buddha discovered an interesting truth on his journey to enlightenment. When he was trying to find ways to diminish the suffering of people, he found that much of the pain wasn't caused by external factors. Instead, it comes from within.

Buddhism follows a set of approaches which helps to get rid of any negativity. Right Approach, right concentration, right speaking, right thought are all parts of what Buddha's teachings. If you start to speak positively to yourself instead of living in a negative state, you eventually reach absolute forgiveness and gain the ability to move on unscathed by any unfortunate events.

Even Jesus – asked his father to forgive those who had crucified him because he knew that underneath it all, none of them really understood the extent of their sin. To forgive is to put aside all thoughts of revenge or anger. When you're able to do just that, you'll achieve absolute forgiveness.

Chapter 6

THE LAW OF FORGIVENESS – HEALING MIND, BODY, RELATIONSHIPS, PERSONAL AND PROFESSIONAL LIFE

⁂

Let's get started by using William's story as an example. William have been working in the bank for many years, hoping that one day he could be the bank manager. However, time and time again, younger men got promoted before he was offered anything. He began to resent everyone around him. He saw them as being favored above him.

LEARN TO SEE THINGS DIFFERENTLY

Things began to change after he took on yoga classes. Not only did yoga brought him health benefits, it taught him valuable life lessons. Since then, he began to look at things differently. When someone was promoted, usually he was resentful, but yoga opened up his mind and he began to accept the realities that he have no control over with. What William didn't realize was that the reason he wasn't promoted was because of his resentment and the way he treated people around him. He was perpetually unhappy and stressed out because he couldn't accept the fact that it was all his fault. Yoga helped him to face his own demons and learned the importance of forgiveness. He had to forgive himself for the negative attitude he had carried with him all his life.

As soon as he changed the way he looked at things and broadened the spectrum of this thoughts, he could see quite clearly that the reason he was always passed over for promotion was because of his performance at work. His colleagues did not think he would be a great leader. He was being seen as someone with bitterness and anger. Within two years of forgiving, he was promoted as a bank manager and it wasn't pure coincidence.

When you see the whole spectrum of

difficulties that are caused by jealousy, hate, greed and negative thought, you also see that it's an obligation to yourself to step beyond negativity toward something more positive.

While you might not believe in Karma, because this is something more associated with the eastern world, you probably know the saying "what goes around comes around," meaning that if you do something wrong, you always get your comeuppance in some way or another.

POWER OF THE LAW OF FORGIVENESS

That's where the power of the law of forgiveness kick in. If you are able to forgive, it empowers you so much that everything seems so positive and you are able to go through life with a whole new viewpoint. We're all human beings. We all make mistakes. We all go through peaks and valleys. Life is never smooth sailing. However, when you learn to use the Law of Forgiveness and make them part of the way you live, you will find happiness and the weight of burden will lighten and disappear.

Earlier in this chapter, I talked about William and when he was asked whether he believed in Karma, he laughed, one of those laughs that is hard to forget – that comes from the heart. Had I asked the same question many years ago, he could not have seen Karma as being something that was valid.

However, ever since he started taking up yoga and meditation classes, he learned the importance of forgiveness. Yoga and meditation helped him to look beyond his narrow spectrum. He soon learned that all his earlier failures in life were caused by the way he treats others and also his closed heart.

Once he understood the Karmic route, he changed his approach to life. He begins to celebrate other people's successes, rather than seeing them as a threat to his own. Things changed for the better when he began to change the way he looked at life. When he learned to let go, the Karmic route of his life changed.

NEVER UNDERESTIMATE THE POWER OF FORGIVENESS

You have the power within you to make that change in your life. Never underestimate the power of forgiveness. The Law of Forgiveness is all about getting things into the right perspective. If someone calls you names, do you see it as an insult? How about seeing that person as being in need of drawing attention to himself and feeling empathy rather than anger? If someone treads on your toe, your toe is quick to recover. However, the injury inside lasts much longer if you can't forgive straight away.

People do things and sometimes the driving power behind those things is their own lives being out of control. When you forgive, you allow them to look at life from a new perspective and sometimes that's all that they need. Show them the bigger picture, rather than the small picture that makes you appear smaller.

Chapter 7

FOCUS ON THE BIGGER PICTURE FROM PERSONAL FORGIVENESS TO WORLD PEACE

It doesn't take much for you to be aware of all of the unhappiness in the world today. And the reason behind all these unhappiness is the lack of understanding and forgiveness.

Now imagine a world where people are able to show empathy and understanding…

Don't you think this is a much better place to live in?

RATE OF HAPPINESS OF COUNTRIES

According to a recent study done on the rate

of happiness of countries from all over the world, Norway, Denmark and Iceland came up as the happiest nations.

The Norwegians, Danish and Icelandic are all nations that are close to nature. They know all about respecting nature and the environment. Schooling is free and healthcare is also universally accepted as being very good. However that wasn't the only criteria. Something different came into play that was every bit as important and that was freedom of choice. Trust and generosity were also among the criteria for finding the happiest country in the world. It is found that the least happy nations of the world were those involved in political turmoil, war and poverty.

Jealousy, greed and all of the other negative feelings that people go through actually unbalance the state of happiness and security. People want more and are perfectly willing to tread over others to get it.

Then, compare this with the world that has left us. Watching TV programs such as Little House on the Prairie takes us back to a time when people's wants and needs were less, but there was less need for social acceptance. If you were poor, then that was okay because someone has to be on the poor end of the scale. If you were rich, you were perhaps respected because of the status of your life and the positive impact you had on people in your community.

So how can we address the balance?
How can we forgive on a national scale?

The answer lies in being as true as you can to your own beliefs while making space in your mind for the beliefs of others.

THINGS WE NEED TO LEARN

We need to learn toleration. We need to learn all about other religions and other races. We need to broaden the spectrum of our lives to be able to put things into perspective. If you haven't thought about how lack of forgiveness is making your life miserable, then you need to look at life from a different perspective, that of compassion. No, we can't save the world from all the wrongdoings but we can change ourselves and lead by example.

In today's world, through social media, the petty jealousies and the close mindedness of the human race are laid out for all to see. You have a choice. You can decide for yourself and learn to forgive life for being so contradictory or you can go with the crowd.

The bigger picture is that life is much more complex than that but so much more simple when you learn the power of forgiveness. When you learn to forgive, you become more compassionate. It can lead you down the path of peace and healing. You learn to let go and move on. You see the value of forgiveness and its importance in your life at a given time. If you are looking forward with dread, it is equally relevant that you are missing out on the opportunities in your life. All over the world, people are suffering. It was the intention of the original Buddha to try to teach people to walk away from their suffering and learn a new way.

Forgiveness is an important part of a full and healthy life. It enables you to begin to build a foundation for your life. A foundation built upon negative thoughts is like building a house in quicksand. You can't do it. If you continue to walk through your life without rectifying the things that you have done wrong, you carry all of that burden with you. If you learn to forgive, you build a solid foundation that can help people around you to trust who you are. Today, we see postings on Facebook where people are judgmental and critical of each other. Tomorrow, we could see hope being spread like its grass seed in a big wind, but it's really up to each individual to start the process. Social media is a powerful way to spread happiness and to share positive views. This is what the world needs now.

FORGIVENESS IS THE KEY TO YOUR HAPPINESS

With natural disasters, fires and loss of life, it is hard to remain stoic, but we have no choice. We cannot change these incidents that come up on the TV each day, but each one of us can change that little part of history that is our lives.

When you learn to forgive, you lead others by example. Never underestimate the power of forgiveness. It is the key to your happiness. It's as simple as that. If you can write down all of the people you need to forgive and then make an active choice to forgive, you will feel better about your life. Not only that, you will begin to notice that your life is changing for the better. Keep on spreading good positive vibes to people around you. Make the world a better place.

Chapter 8

WHAT HOLDS YOU BACK FROM FORGIVING

Let's take a look at what is happening around us today. We all expect to live in homes that are fully equipped. We expect to have all the latest technology, designer label clothing and to have a quality of lifestyle that we consider we deserve.

However, regardless of what the TV tells you about being worth all this expense, you are losing something fundamentally important to your life by living the American dream as it currently stands. That's not to say that the original American Dream wasn't a bad idea. It was based upon principles that are easy to understand but it wasn't about whether you own the latest model of iPhone.

BLAME VS FORGIVENESS

What has happened over the years is that you have become complacent. It's easier to blame than to forgive. It's easier to look at life and ask what's in it for you, rather than understanding that the greatest things you can expect from life actually come from being able to forgive. I have been watching social media very closely while coming up with ideas for this book and it worries me that people go through their lives looking for someone to blame for the quality of their lives.

Let me give you an example. If the schooling system isn't working, it's the fault of the government. If the operation didn't turn out like it should have, it's the fault of the surgeon. We live in a society that takes responsibility very seriously although we have forgotten how to take personal responsibility. People always ask "What's in it for me?" and the only way that you can ever experience what there is in forgiveness for you is to actually forgive.

There are times when you struggle in life, I mean we all do right? But what's important is that instead of pushing blames or pointing fingers at others, learn to do some self reflection.

IMPLEMENT FORGIVENESS INTO YOUR EVERYDAY LIFE

Most of the times, it's the way we look at things, how we react and deal with pain and hardships in our lives. Perhaps, life would be much easier for you if you could see it from a different perspective. Instead of implementing forgiveness into your everyday life, it is also important to be grateful for what you have.

- Did you know that around 22,000 children die each day due to poverty?
- Did you know that a child dies from hunger-related diseases every 10 seconds?
- Did you know that 603 million people lack access to clean water?

Take some time to do some self examination by asking yourself these questions:

- How did I contribute to this situation?
- What can I do to make the situation better?

- What can I do to show people I love them?
- What does it matter who says sorry?

And then ask yourself the obvious question: What's in it for me?

You'll be fulfilled knowing that you had already done the best you could and leave no regrets. You'll also discover the freedom that can be achieved by a simple act of forgiveness. Forgive yourself and forgive others for their seemingly thoughtless actions. When you learn to let go, you open up the potential to have great relationships and to feel spiritually awakened.

You can never discover the best version of you until you are able to let go and forgive. Let's finish this chapter with some quotations on forgiveness that will help you to see the benefits for yourself, from different perspectives.

"To be a Christian means to forgive the inexcusable because God has forgiven the inexcusable in you." – C. S. Lewis

"The truth is, unless you let go, unless you

forgive yourself, unless you forgive the situation, unless you realize that the situation is over, you cannot move forward." – Steve Maraboli

"True forgiveness is when you can say, "Thank you for that experience." - Oprah Winfrey

"Forgiveness has nothing to do with absolving a criminal of his rime. It has everything to do with relieving oneself of the burden of being a victim--letting go of the pain and transforming oneself from victim to survivor." – C. R. Strahan

You can also look up some quotations on your own and make them part of your daily mantra when you wake up in the morning. This will constantly remind you that it is the first step toward a more loving and positive relationship with yourself, and therefore with others.

Chapter 9

PRAYER FOR FORGIVENESS

Whether we are seeking forgiveness of our sins or asking God to help us forgive others, prayer is the first place to start when seeking restoration and healing.

Says this prayer of forgiveness.

Lord Jesus, for too long I've kept you out of my life. I know that i am a sinner and that I cannot save myself. No longer will I close the door when I hear you knocking. By faith I gratefully receive your gift of Salvation. I am ready to trust you as my Lord and Saviour. Thank you, Lord Jesus, for coming to earth. I believe you are the Son of God who died on the cross for my sins and rose from the dead on the third day. Thank you for bearing my sins and giving me the gift of eternal life. I believe your words are true. Come into my heart, Lord Jesus, and be my saviour. Amen.

PRAYER FOR FORGIVING OTHERS

Dear Merciful Lord,
Thank you for your gift of firgiveness. Your Only son loved me enough to come to earth and experience the worst pain imaginable so i could be forgiven. Your Mercy flows to me in spite of my faults and failures. Your Word says to *"clothe yourselves with love, which binds us all together in perfect harmony. "(Col. 3:14)* Help me demonstrate unconditional love today, even to those who hurt me.

I understand that even though I feel scarred, my emotions don't have to control my actions. Father, may your sweet words saturate my mind and direct my thoughts. Help me to release the hurt and begin to love as Jesus loves. I want to see my offender through my saviour's eyes. If I can be forgiven, so can he. I understand there are no levels to your love. We are all your children, and your desire is that none of us should perish.

You teach us to *"let the peace that comes from Christ rule in our hearts."* *(Col.3:15)* When I forgive in words, allow your Holy Spirit to fill my heart with peace. I am thankful always, with gratitude I can come closer to you and let go of unforgiveness. With gratitude I can see the person who caused my pain as a child of the Most High God. Loved and accepted. Help me find the compassion that comes with true forgiveness.

PRAYER TO FORGIVE YOURSELF

Father, today I ask for forgiveness of all the negative and harmful words I have spoken about myself. I do not want to abuse myself in such a way again. Transform my thoughts and let me understand how marvelous you made me. Change my habits so I use my tonque to speak hope and favour upon my life. In Jesus Mighty Name

PRAYER TO FORGIVE OTHERS

Dear Lord. I thank you for the power of forgiveness, and I choose to forgive everyone who has hurt me. Help me set everyone who has offended me free and release them to you (Roman 12:19)

Help me walk in righteousness, peace, and joy as I choose to be kind and compassionate, forgiving others, just as You forgave me in Jesus Name.

CONCLUSION

Once you understand the process of forgiveness, it's time for you to use it to make the world that you live in a better place.

You'll be stronger, more compassionate and empathetic. The wonderful thing about being able to let go and forgive is that it'll also make a major impact on the lives of people you love. Nonetheless, this habit will also benefit your social and business life.

Let's do some self-discovery. Go ahead and ask yourself these questions:

- Who had wronged you in the past?
- What attempt have you made to forgive them?
- What is it that you cannot forgive yourself for?

doesn't matter as long as you keep making progress to achieve true happiness and freedom deep within.

Who haven't you called for a long time? Make that call and make it about that person, rather than about yourself. Show your interest in the lives of others and become more compassionate in the process. If the last time you wronged this person in the past, let him/her know that you are sorry and mean it. Forgive yourself. Stop holding your life back all the time.

Stop living in your head and get beyond it. If this means facing your demons one at a time, then do so. Write down what you did that was so wrong and forgive yourself for it, unconditionally. After all, we're just humans and we do mistakes. Learn from it and start focusing on things that really matter.

Forgiveness is a wonderful value to pass on to your children. But here's the irony, children are actually better at forgiving than most adults! Think about it, we often ask our children to shake hands with kids they have fallen out with and say "Sorry" – So why can't you?

Never stop practicing forgiveness. Remember to recognize what's in it for you. It's the best gift that you can ever give yourself and life is too short to hold onto the unnecessary grudges.

Here's my last question for you:

Do you want to experience more bitterness or happiness in your life?

Today is the day for you to find the Freedom in Forgiveness.